USN AIRCR
1922 - 1962

VOL. 7

TYPE DESIGNATION LETTER 'F'
PART FOUR

PHIL H. LISTEMANN

NOTAM:

This study was undertaken using the available movement cards of each USN aircraft in service between 1922 and 1962.
These cards may occasionally contain errors which could lead to some disparities or omissions when the text below is compared with official or non-official publications already published.
Alphabetical order has been chosen to structure the book (except sometimes for prototype), rather than the chronological order of introduction into USN/USMC/USCG service.
Unless otherwise noted, the photographs come from the USN or from sources such as the National Archives or National Museum of Naval Aviation.

ISBN: 979-1096490-42-4

Copyright

© 2019 Philedition - Phil Listemann

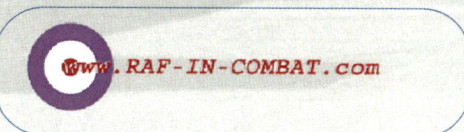
www.RAF-IN-COMBAT.com

Over forty years, between 1922 and 1962, the USN and USMC used a designation system which began with biplanes and ended with jets, having been used through two major wars, WW2 and the Korean War. This system remained largely the same during that time, though it evolved with the introduction of new types and technology, and new exceptions developed as well. The purpose of this series is to explain this system using photographs.

On 18 September 1962, a new system was introduced that was common to the three air arms (USAF, Army and USN/USMC) and which is still in force today. The application of this Tri-service system was effective immediately for aircraft pending delivery to the USN, but took a couple of weeks to be implemented fully in the case of aircraft already accepted, especially for aircraft based overseas or cruising on aircraft carriers.

The designation system was based on:

1 - A type designation which describes the basic mission of the aircraft.

2 - A letter designating the manufacturer (but not necessarily the designer) following the type designation.

3 - A configuration sequence indicating minor change to the aircraft type, the initial model being designated '1'.

4 - Manufacturer type sequence.

5 - Status prefix. Only two letters were assigned, 'X' - Experimental - and 'Y' - Service test - from 1951 onwards.

6 - Special Purpose Suffix which indicates an aircraft used in a special configuration.

Samples:

AD-6: Douglas First Attack type, sixth model.

F2A-1: Brewster Second Fighter type, initial model.

A3D-2P: Douglas Third Attack type, second model, reconnaissance version.

PB4Y-1: Consolidated Fourth Patrol Bomber type, initial model.

TYPE DESIGNATION

A	Ambulance	1943-1946			Patrol	1923-1962
	Attack	1946-1962		PB	Patrol-Bomber	1935-1962
B	Bomber	1931-1943		PTB	Patrol, Torpedo-Bomber	1937
BF	Bomber-Fighter	1934-1937		R	Racer	1922-1928
BT	Bomber-Torpedo	1942-1945		R	Transport	1931-1962
DS	Anti-Submarine Drone	1959-1962		RO	Rotorcycle	1954-1959
F	Fighter	1922-1962		S	Anti-Submarine	1951-1962
G	Transport, Single-Engined	1939-1941		SB	Scout-Bomber	1934-1946
	Inflight refuelling Tanker	1958-1962		SN	Scout-Trainer	1939-1962
H	Hospital	1929-1943		SO	Scout-Observation	1934-1946
	Helicopter	1943-1962		T	Torpedo	1922-1935
J	Transport	1926-1931			Transport	1927-1930
	General Utility	1931-1955			Trainer	1948-1962
JR	Utility Transport	1935-1955		TB	Torpedo-Bomber	1935-1946
L	Glider	1941-1945		TD	Target Drone	1942-1946
M	Marine Expeditionary	1922-1923		TS	Torpedo-Scout	1943
N	Trainer	1922-1960		U	Utility	1955-1962
O	Observation	1922-1962			Unpiloted Drone	1946-1955
OS	Observation Scout	1935-1945		W	Electronic Search	1952-1962
P	Pursuit	1923				

MANUFACTURERS CODE

A	Aeromarine	1922			Cessna	1943		Gould	1942-1945
	Atlantic (Fokker)	1927-1930			De Havilland Canada	1955-1956		Pratt-Read	1942-1945
	General Aviation	1930-1932		CH	Caspar-Werke	1922		Edo	1943-1946
	Brewster	1935-1943		D	Douglas	1922-1962		Hiller	1948-1962
	Allied (Gliders only)	1941-1943			McDonnell	1942-1946		Cessna	1951-1962
	Noorduyn	1946			Radioplane	1943-1962	F	Fokker	1922
B	Aerial	1922			Frankfort	1945-1946		Grumman	1931-1962
	Boeing	1923-1959		DH	De Havilland	1927-1931		Fairchild Canada	1942-1945
	Beechcraft	1937-1945		DW	Dayton-Wright	1922-1923	G	Gallaudet	1922
	Budd	1942-1944		E	Elias	1922-1924		Eberhart	1927-1928
BS	Blackburn	1922			Detroit	1928		Great Lakes	1929-1936
C	Curtiss	1922-1946			Bellanca	1931-1937		Aga Aviation	1942
	Culver	1943-1946			Piper	1941-1945		Goodyear	1942-1962

	Globe	1946-1959		Spartan	1940-1941	**W**	Wright	1922-1926
H	Huff-Daland	1941-1945		Piper (gliders)	1942-1943		Waco	1934-1945
	Hall	1928-1940		Piasecki	1946-1962		CCF	1942-1945
	Stearman-Hammond	1937-1938	**PL**	Parnall	1922	**X**	Cox-Klemin	1922-1924
	Howard	1941-1944	**Q**	Ward Hall	1926	**Y**	Consolidated	1926-1962
	Snead	1942		Stinson	1934-1936		Vultee-Stinson	1942-1945
	McDonnell	1946-1962		Fairchild	1928-1962	**Z**	Pennsylvania Airc.	1933-1934
HP	Handley Page	1922		Bristol Aeronautical	1941-1943			
J	Berliner-Joyce	1929-1935	**R**	Ford	1927-1932			
	General Aviation	1935		Maxson-Brewster	1939-1940			
	North American	1937-1962		Ryan	1941-1946			
JL	Junkers-Larson	1922		Aeronca	1942			
K	JV Martin	1922-1924		American	1942			
	Keystone	1927-1930		Brunswick	1942-1943			
	Kreider-Reisner	1935-1936		Interstate	1942-1962			
	Kinner	1935-1936		Radioplane	1943-1962			
	Fairchild	1937-1942	**RO**	Meridionali-Romeo	1933			
	Nash-Kelvinator	1942	**S**	Stout	1922			
	Kaiser-Fleetwings	1943-1945		Sikorsky	1928-1962			
	Kaman	1950-1962		Sterman	1934-1945			
L	LWF	1922		Schweizer	1941			
	Loening	1924-1933		Supermarine	1943			
	Bell	1939-1962		Sperry	1950			
	Langley	1942-1943	**T**	Thomas-Morse	1922			
	Columbia	1945		New Standard	1930-1934			
M	Martin	1922-1962		Northrop	1933-1944			
	General Motors	1942-1945		Timm	1941-1943			
	McCulloch	1953-1954		Taylorcraft	1942			
N	NAF	1922-1945		Temco	1956			
	Gyrodyne	1960	**U**	Vought	1922-1962			
O	Viking	1929-1936	**V**	Vultee	1941			
	Lockheed	1931-1950		Lockheed-Vega	1942-1962			
	Piper	1960		Vickers Canada	1943-1945			
P	Pitcairn	1931-1932	**VK**	Vickers	1922			

SPECIAL PURPOSE SUFFIX

A	Amphibious, Armament (on normally unarmed aircraft), Arrester-gear (on non-carried aircraft), USAAF contract, Land-based version of carrier aircraft, Miscellaneous modification.	**N**	Night fighter, All-weather radar
		NA	Night fighter modified for day attack
		NL	Night fighter modified for cold-weather operations
B	British contracts (Lend-Lease), Special armament, Miscellanous modification.	**P**	Photographic
		Q	Electronic countermeasures
C	Cannon-armed, Stressed for catapulting, Arrested gear added.	**R**	Transport conversion

CP	Photographic survey (Trimtrogen camera)	**S**	Seaplane	
D	Drone director, Drop tanks		Anti-Submarine (killer)	1951-1962
E	Electronic equipment	**T**	Trainer version	1934-1946
F	Flagship, re-engined version	**U**	Utility version	1939-1962
G	USCG version, Gunned version (on unarmed aircraft)	**W**	Anti-Submarine (hunter), Early Warning	
H	Hospital (Ambulance)	**Z**	Staff transport	
J	Cold-weather equipment			
K	Drone conversion			
KD	Radio-controlled drone			
L	Winterised, Searchlight carrier			
M	Missile launcher			

F

FIGHTER
(1922 - 1962)

TYPE
FF, F2F, F3F, F4F, F5F

XFF-1

-

X: Experimental, **F:** Fighter, **F:** Grumman First type, **1:** Initial model
Grumman first fighter type, prototype of the initial model

Number of aircraft ordered: 1
Number of aircraft accepted: -
Delivery dates: -
Last stricken date: -

Bu.No:
A-8878 (1)

In the late 1920s Grumman was only known as a float designer, and manufacturer, for US Navy types like the Loening amphibian. However, the Grumman team had been thinking about designing an aircraft for the USN, but had not had the opportunity to do so. This eventually came in 1930 when the company became aware of a requirement for a two-seat fighter that included a request from the Bureau of Aeronautics (BuAer) to see if the new retractable undercarriage designed by Grumman could be adapted to existing carrier fighters such as the Boeing F4B and Curtiss F8C. Grumman was reluctant to let others benefit from its successful engineering design so decided to attempt to fulfil the requirement for a new Navy fighter. The new design was submitted in March 1930 and the BuAer immediately expressed great interest in it. Because of a lack of funds, and also because Grumman was a newcomer to the field, the project did not get underway for a year when a contract was signed on 28 March 1931 for one prototype, with the USN designation XFF-1 and allocated BuNo A-8878.

The XFF-1 made its first flight on 29 December 1931 powered by a 575-hp Wright R-1820-E radial driving a two-blade ground-adjustable propeller that gave a top speed of 195 mph, 7 mph faster than the Boeing F4B! It also incorporated an enclosed cockpit, with dual sliding canopies, and a fully retractable main landing gear. The prototype was of all-metal construction, which was relatively new for its time, although the wings were fabric covered. The armament of the XFF-1 was conventional with two forward firing 0.30-in calibre machine guns complemented by a single machine-gun, on a flexible mount, in the rear cockpit. The XFF-1 was tested at Anacostia, but later lost its experimental status in October 1932, after it was modified by contract during the summer, and was actually accepted as an **FF-1**.

Grumman XFF-1 at Anacostia for Navy trials during the winter of 1931 - 1932. This was the first aircraft in a long dynasty of Grumman naval fighters. At that time the usage of the letter 'A' in the BuNo had been discontinued.

Above and below FF-1 BuNo 8878 in flight and exposing various details on the retractable undercarriage. At that time BuNo had been re-engined with a more powerful 750-hp R-1820-F and because of this and with other modifications incorporated, the aircraft had the 'X' removed from its designation being actually similar to a production FF-1. BuNo was officially accepted in February 1933 and was lost in a flying accident in March 1937.

FF-1

-

F: Fighter, F: Grumman First type, 1: Initial model
Grumman first fighter type, initial model

Number of aircraft ordered:	**27**
Number of aircraft accepted:	**28** *(including one conversion from XFF-1)*
Delivery dates:	**Apr.33/Nov.33** *(Feb.33 for ex-XFF-1)*
Last stricken date:	*n/a*

Bu.No:
8878 (1), **9350-9376** (27)

The test flights of the XFF-1 were satisfactory and eventually led to an order for 27 production aircraft on 19 December 1932 under the designation of FF-1. The production version was similar to the FF-1 BuNo 8878, with its final modifications, the engine now being the Wright R-1820-78, the military version of the R-1820-F.

The number ordered was enough to equip a single Fighting Squadron and the unit selected was VF-5B on the USS *Lexington*. The FF-1 replaced the Boeing F4B in this squadron. The unit began to receive its new aircraft in June 1933 and served until the autumn of 1935 when it was reassigned to the USS *Ranger*. By November 1935, VF-5B lost half of its FFs and received nine F2F-1s as a temporary measure pending the arrival of new F3F-1s. These arrived in March and April 1936, after which the FF was withdrawn from frontline service. During the three years VF-5B operated the type, none were lost in accidents, an incredibly good safety record for a military aircraft of that time. By the spring of 1936, 25 FF-1s were still serving with the USN and all surviving airframes were converted to **FF-2** configuration by the Naval Aircraft Factory in Philadelphia.

FF-1 BuNo 9363 just before touching down the deck. It was a phase the pilots were not very comfortable with because the FF-1 had a tendency to bounce on touching down.

The first FF-1 to be assigned to Fighting Squadron Five (VF-5B) was BuNo 9351, which is seen at the factory, with freshly painted codes 5-F-1 for the Squadron's leader. But the cowling has yet to be painted.

FF-1 BuNo 9358 warming up while serving with VF-5B. As aircraft #8, the upper part of the cowling should have been painted blue, but it is not the case here, and the cowling is probably a new one and was still to be painted.

FF-1 BuNo 9362/5-F-12 . As with #12 it belongs to the fourth (Black) section.

BuNo 9369 was initially stored before being issued to VF-5B in January 1934 as replacement aircraft.

BuNo 9367 was one the 18 FF-1s assigned to VF-5B when the type was introduced into service. It was later converted to FF-2 standard.

FF-1 BuNo 9368 served with Fighting Squadron Five between January 1934 and April 1936 when it was sent to the Naval Aircraft Factory where it was converted as an FF-2.

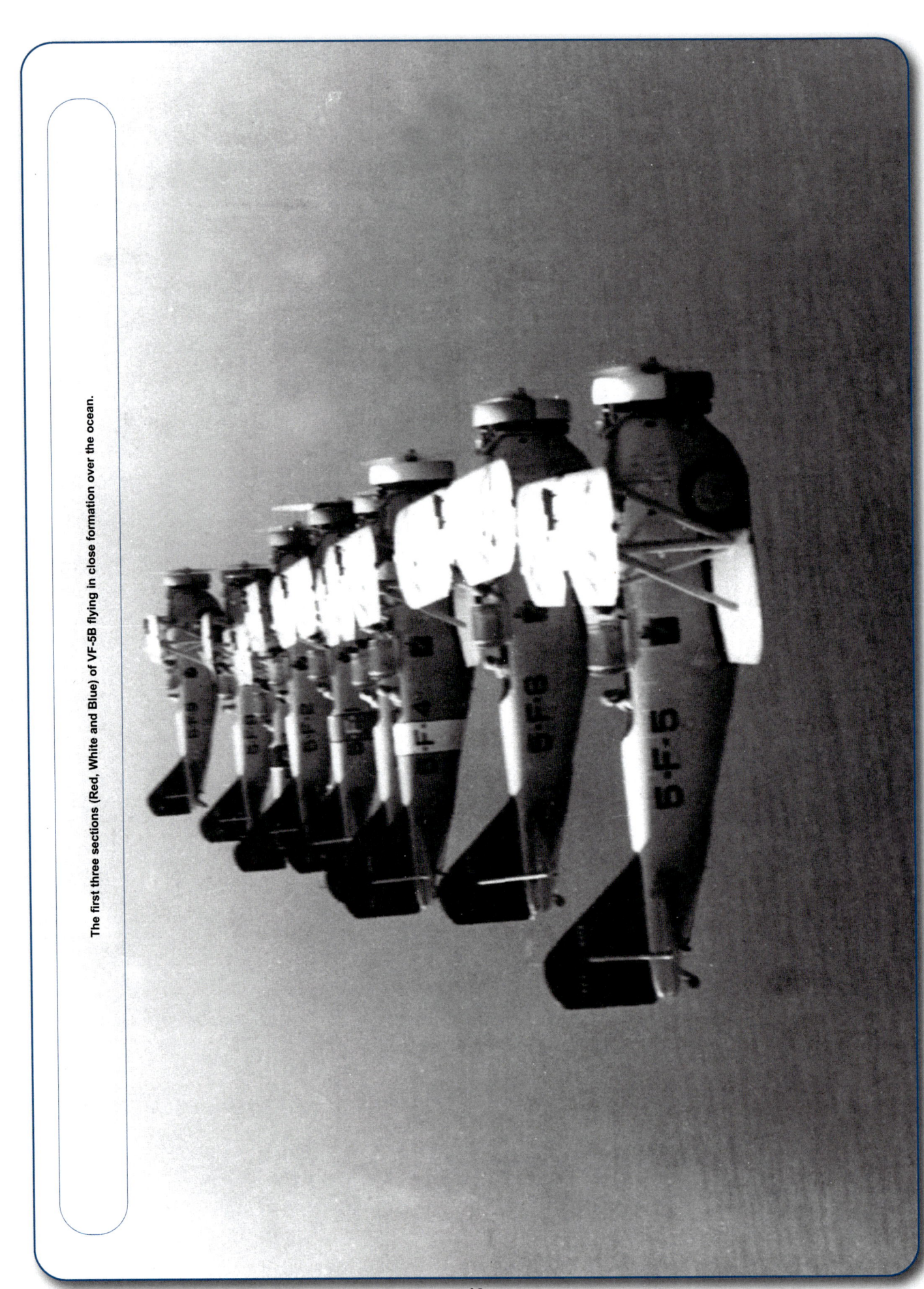

The first three sections (Red, White and Blue) of VF-5B flying in close formation over the ocean.

FF-2

-

F: Fighter, **F**: Grumman First type, **2**: Second model
Grumman first fighter type, second model

Number of aircraft ordered: **25** *(conversions from FF-1 airframe)*
Number of aircraft accepted: **25**
Delivery dates: **Feb.36/Sep.36**
Last stricken date: **Jul.42**

Bu.No:
9350-9359, 9362-9376

Intended for use as fighter trainers, the FF-2s were fitted with dual flight controls and, as they were not intended to be used on aircraft carriers, the tail hook was removed. All FF-2s were converted from existing FF-1 airframes and the first were sent to the Naval Aircraft Factory for modifications in the autumn of 1935. The forward firing machine guns were normally retained, but there were exceptions. An exhaust collector ring was fitted in place of the individual exhaust stacks used on the FF-1. Finally, radios were installed in all of the aircraft that were not already so equipped.

After conversion to FF-2s, the aircraft were distributed among the various Naval Reserve Aviation Bases (NRAB) across the country. In some cases the aircraft were pooled when a USN Reserve unit and a USMC Reserve unit were located at the same base. They were used to give refresher courses to reserve pilots or pilots temporarily posted to non-flying duties. Some, at a later time in their career, were used as liaison aircraft for bases or units. The FF-2 continued to be used to train pilots until the attack on Pearl Harbor and, by December 1941, only seven aircraft remained in the USN inventory as many aircraft never received an authorisation for overhaul and had been withdrawn from service when this came due. With the outbreak of war, and the increasing availability of more modern trainers, the FF-2s ceased to be of practical use and the final withdrawal of the type took place in July 1942.

The engine of BuNo 9356 is warming up for a test flight after its conversion to an FF-2 at the Naval Aircraft Factory in April 1936. Tactical markings have not yet been applied.

Above, after its conversion to FF-2, BuNo 9356 served at the NRAB Kansas City as #2. The tail and stabilisers are white.

Below BuNo 9362 seen after being converted to FF-2 standard. Note the rudder stripes of the reserve aircraft, but the FF-2s were rarely painted like this.

Above, the Leader of the third (Blue) section was flying this FF-2 BuNo 9364 with a blue cowling and fuselage band. The tail is believed to be red. Note the Reserve insignia which was painted under the gunner's seat. The location of the insignia varied from one aircraft from another.

Below and middle, Grumman FF-2 BuNo 9371 believed to have served with NRAB Glenview in 1937. There is no Reserve insignia painted on this aircraft however. At the end of its career, BuNo 9371 served as liaison aircraft # 5 for NAS Norfolk, thence the inscription "NAS NORFOLK" painted on the fuselage. The aircraft was left in bare metal.

Just after their conversion to FF-2, BuNos 9372 and 9376 were allocated to NRAB Minneapolis and were respectively the second and third taken on charge by this NRAB, the first being BuNo 9369. The section colours for reserve units were normally the same as fleet units. This seems to be the case here, and consequently BuNo 9376 should be #3 with its lower part of its cowling painted red. *(National Archives)*

XF2F-1

-

X: Experimental, **F**: Fighter, **2F**: Grumman Second type, **1**: Initial model
Grumman second fighter type, prototype of the initial model

Number of aircraft ordered:	**1**
Number of aircraft accepted:	**1**
Delivery dates:	**May.34**
Last stricken date:	**Apr.38**
Bu.No:	
9342 (1)	

In 1932, the USN was already looking at a fighter to replace the Boeing F4B and the Grumman FF, the latter about to be introduced into service. In response to this, Grumman submitted a new design that was a small, single-seat biplane with an enclosed cockpit and a retractable landing gear similar to that used on the FF-1. Power was to be provided by a 625-hp Pratt & Whitney R-1535-44 Twin Wasp Jr air-cooled radial engine. Impressed with the potential of the Grumman design, the USN ordered a single prototype on 2 November 1934 as the XF2F-1.

The XF2F-1 first flew on 18 October 1933 and had fabric-covered wings and a metal fuselage skin. The armament was conventional for the time with two 0.30-in calibre machine guns in the forward fuselage. The first trials led to some minor modifications, especially around the engine. With these changes, the aircraft continued the flight test programme, leading to an order of a production version in May 1934 at the same time the XF2F-1 was officially accepted by the Navy. The XF2F-1 continued to fly until an accident on 12 April 1938 and it was struck from the inventory.

Side view of the XF2F-1 in October 1934. It is seen with the modifications undertaken after the initials trials. Also newly installed, a large antenna located just forward of the vertical fin and a telescopic gun sight.

Two views of the XF2F-1 in flight with gear retracted and gear down. At that time this device was still new enough to be exposed to the camera.

F2F-1

-

F: Fighter, **2F**: Grumman Second type, **1**: Initial model
Grumman second fighter type, initial model.

Number of aircraft ordered:	54
Number of aircraft accepted:	55
Delivery dates:	Jan.35/Aug.35
Last stricken date:	Feb.43

Bu.No:
9623/9676 (54), **9997** (1)

Following the conclusion of the prototype's testing, the USN placed an order for 54 F2F-1s in May 1934. Very similar to the prototype, the engine was the R-1535-72 variant, a different propeller was installed and other minor changes incorporated. An additional machine was built to replace an earlier built example that crashed on delivery to the USN.

The first unit to be equipped with the new fighter was VF-2B, which later became VF-2, and embarked on the USS *Lexington*. It eventually became the main user of the type and relinquished its last F2F in October 1940. The unit was followed by VF-3B on the USS *Ranger*. Again, this squadron was later designated VF-7B and, subsequently VF-5, and embarked on the USS *Yorktown*. At the time, the F2F constituted the mainstay of the fighter units of the Battle force, but soon lost this supremacy when its successor, the F3F, was introduced in 1936. Nevertheless, the F2F-1 soldiered on until the introduction of the F2A. At that time, in 1940, the F2F was totally obsolete and, no matter the opponent, had no chance in aerial combat. The career of the F2F-1 continued at Pensacola (Naval Training Center – Fixed Gunnery School) and as an advanced fighter trainer at Miami and reserve units where it suffered a high attrition rate in the hands of air cadets. By Pearl Harbor, about two dozen were still in the USN inventory, many having been withdrawn from use in previous months after reaching their airframe hours limit. With the war, the demand for new fighter pilots was huge and they needed to be trained on more modern aircraft. Because of that, and to standardise the fleet, the last F2F-1s were stricken from the USN inventory list in February 1943.

Fighting Squadron Two was the first squadron to be operational of F2F1s. Here the Green Section leader is flying on F2F-1 BuNo 9636 which flew until being stricken in February 1943.

F2F-1 BuNo 9652 taken in flight as 2-F-6 (2nd Section - White) in 1939. This airframe served with VF-3B and VF-5B and would end its career at NRAB Chicago. AS many aircraft of this type, it was stricken in at the end of February 1943. Note that only the last three digits of the BuNo are visible. The '9' has been either over-painted or censored. The tail is white (USS *Saratoga*).

Middle, Grumman F2F-1 BuNo 9630 which was issued to VF-5B in 1935 and was coded 2-F-8 (3rd Section - Blue) and was part of the USS *Lexington* Air Group (tail color Yellow). By Pearl Harbor, BuNo 9630 was serving as advanced trainer at NAS Miami and was stricken soon after in April 1942.

Below, BuNo 9633 became the air-craft of 4th Section (Black) when it was issued the VF-2B in 1935. It later served as advanced trainer at NAS Miami until the end of December 1942 when it was stricken.

F2F-1s of the 2nd Section (White) flying in formation in 1939. Behind BuNo 9652 (see previous page), F2F-1 coded 2-F-4 is BuNo 9675 which served long enough to become an advanced trainer at NAS Miami until April 1942. The third aircraft coded 2-F-5 cannot be identified as his BuNo (as well its denomination) has been erased. It was probably a new comer and only the tail has been painted in white so far.

Above F2F-1 BuNo 9635 of the 4th Section (Black). It served the USN until the end of April 1942 when it was stricken. It was serving at that time at NAS Miami as advanced trainer. Below, F2F-1 BuNo 9637 of the 5th Section (Green) had a similar career to BuNo 9635. Both were initially issued to VF-2B in March 1935.

Above F2F-1 BuNo 9640 of the 6th Section (Yellow) seen in July 1935. It later lost while serving as an advanced trainer at NAS Miami on 21 August 1941 when it entered into an involuntary inverted spin while the pilot was attempting aerobatics and was abandoned. Below F2F-1 BuNo 9624 wearing the colours of the leader of the 1st Section of VF-3 and part of the USS *Ranger* Air Group (Green tail). This F2F served previously with VF-2B. BuNo 9624 was lost in a flying accident at Miami on 22 February 1942 in the same circumstances as BuNo 9640 above. Involuntary spin was a regular flaw noticed on the F2F.

Above Grumman F2F-1s of the 3rd Section of VF3-B are starting their engines for another training flight in 1935. In the forefront, BuNo 9653/3-F-8 which was part of the initial betch issued to Fighting Squadron Three. Behind, F2F-1 BuNo 9654 that was lost by accident on 30 January 1937. It was replaced by BuNo 9626 below, an aircraft which had been initially issued to VF-2B.

In July 1937, Fighting Squadron VF-7B was re-designated VF-5. Grumman F2F-1 BuNo 9672 above was coded 5-F-1 and therefore was the aircraft flown by the leader of the 1st Section (Red). Below, BuNo 9666 became the first aircraft of the 3rd Section (Blue) as 5-F-8. Both aircraft were later passed on to NAS Miami to serve as advanced trainer and were stricken from inventory in April 1942 and November 1942 respectively. The tail is painted on red (USS *Yorktown*)

Grumman F2F-1 BuNo 9664 on the deck of USS Yorktown. Later serving at NAS Miami as advanced trainer it was finally stricken in April 1942. *(National Archives)*

Serving on the USS *Wasp*, Fighting Squadron Seven received some F2Fs in complement of its F3Fs when it was commissioned in July 1939. Here BuNo 9641 coded 7-F-12 wearing the Neutrality Patrol roundel ahead of the cockpit. BuNo 9641 was stricken at the end of December 1942.

Built as replacement to BuNo 9634 which had crashed on delivery, BuNo 997 was the last F2F-1 built and after a short service with VF-5B and VF-2B, it was issued to the VF-4M and was lost in a crash on 29 May 1937 killing its pilot. The USMC used a handful of F2Fs as interim aircraft.

On 1 July 1937, VF-4M of the USMC saw its designation changing to VMF-2. BuNo 9663 is now wearing the new codes. BuNo was not more luckier than BuNo 9997 above as it was also lost by accident a few weeks late on 30 November 1937.

XF3F-1

-

Number of aircraft ordered:	**1**
Number of aircraft accepted:	**1**
Delivery dates:	**Aug.35**
Last stricken date:	**Feb.43**

Bu.No:
9727 (3)

As the F2F was experiencing some shortcomings, Grumman was awarded a contract in October 1934 for a single prototype to rectify the situation. The new type received the denomination XF3F-1 with BuNo 9727.

Basically, the XF3F-1 was an improved F2F incorporating relatively simple modifications to correct the directional stability problem and excessive tendency to spin that had been encountered with the F2F. The airframe was lengthened and the wings were larger, but the aircraft was still powered by the same engine, the P&W R-1535 of 650-hp, but now the dash 72 variant. The prototype flew for the first time on 20 March 1935, but crashed two days later, killing its pilot. It was immediately replaced by a second prototype with the same Bureau Number and made its maiden flight on 9 May 1935. It was also lost a few days later, the pilot baling out. A third prototype, again with the same BuNo, was built and flew on 7 June 1935, but incorporated a larger rudder to improve spin recovery characteristics. The trials were conducted without major incident and led to the acceptance of the aircraft for the USN.

After completion of the trials, the XF3F-1 was initially sent to NAS Anacostia to serve as a station aircraft before reaching Miami where it served as an advanced trainer from mid-1941 until being stricken in February 1943.

The first of the three XF3F-1 prototypes seen on the grass field at the Grumman plant of Farmingdale on 20 March 1935. It was destroyed two days later.

F3F-1

-

F: Fighter, **3F**: Grumman Third type, **1**: Initial model
Grumman third fighter type, initial model.

Number of aircraft ordered:	**54**
Number of aircraft accepted:	**55** *(including one conversion from XF3F-2)*
Delivery dates:	**Mar.36/Sep.36** *(Apr.38 for ex-XF3F-2)*
Last stricken date:	**Jul.43**

Bu.No:
0211/0264 (54), **0452** (1)

Despite the early misadventures, the USN ordered 54 F3F-1s on 24 August 1935 to equip two squadrons. Production differed little from the third prototype. The engine was the dash 84 instead of the dash 72, the starboard 0.30-in calibre machine gun was replaced by the more powerful 0.50-in calibre weapon and the propeller was a Hamilton Standard in place of the original Lycoming Smith unit. Fighting Squadron Five (VF-5B, re-named VF-4 after 1 July 1937) was the first to transition to the F3F-1, followed by VF-6B (renamed VF-3 in July 1937). In the following months, more fighter squadrons received the F3F-1. Before Pearl Harbor, further fighter squadrons received the F3F-1: VF-2, VF-5 (ex-VF-3B), VF-6, VF-7 and VMF-2 of the USMC. The F3F-1s continued to serve in frontline units until early 1941 and were then sent to Training Command at Miami or Norfolk. This first phase of usage was paved by many accidents and sixteen F3F-1s were written off while serving in the frontline units, a rather high attrition rate even considering the standards of the time.

By early 1943, the surviving airframes were reaching their limits and the type was progressively retired. By 1 January 1943, the fleet included nineteen aircraft, but, one by one, they were struck from the inventory. The last F3F-1, BuNo 0235, was eventually retired in July 1943.

F3F-1 BuNo 0232 served with VF-4 between September and November 1940. Damaged in an accident, it was repaired and then sent to train fighter pilots at Miami. It was finally stricken in November 1942.

Above, F3F-1 BuNo 0259 was assigned to Fighting Squadron Six (VF-6B) on delivery, a squadron which took the denomination of Fighting Squadron Three (VF-3) on 1 July 1937, still belonging to the air group embarked on the USS *Saratoga* (white tail). BuNo 0259 is wearing the colors of the VF-3 Blue Section Leader. This F3F-1 later served with VF-4 and VF-71 and then as an advanced trainer at Miami until being in an accident in February 1942.

Below, BuNo 0221 had a short career with the USN as it was lost while serving with Fighting Squadron Five (VF-5B) on the USS *Ranger* (Blue tail). This airframe on lost by accident on 10 November 1936 with 236.4 hours logged. The fuselage band and cowling are black, and 0221 was the aircraft flown by the leader of the Black Section. *(National Naval Aviation Museum)*

First Section of VF-4 (Red cowling) flying in formation. This squadron named was before July 1937, Fighting Squadron Five (VF-5B). The tail color was changed from Blue to Green. VF-4 was part of the USS *Ranger* air group.
Below F3F-1 BuNo 0253 of the Black Section leader. BuNo 0253 was eventually stricken in January 1943. *(National Naval Aviation Museum)*

Left, F3F-1 BuNo 0231 of the Red Section of Fighting Squadron Six (later VF-3 in July 1937). This airframe ended its career as many others as an advanced trainer at Miami and was stricken in February 1943.

F3F-1 BuNo 0239 of the same unit wearing the colors of the Black Section leader. As for 0231, it last assignment was NAS Miami to train fighter pilots and stricken one month after 0231.
(National Naval Aviation Museum)

F3F-1 BuNo 0247 had a shorter career in being lost in a an accident in October 1936. It was part of the Yellow Section of VF6-B.

F3F-1 BuNo 0239 was used initially by VF6B/VF-3. Then it was assigned to Fighting Squadron Seven (USS Wasp) in December 1939 and served with the squadron until October 1940 before ending its days as an advanced trainer at Miami until March 1943.

The Marines were not a big user of the F3F-1 with half of dozen aircraft only and this for a short time in 1937 with Marine Fighting Squadron Four which was renamed VMF-2 in July 1937. The type was used as an interim equipment while awaiting delivery of the F3F-2. However BuNo 251 had a short career with the Marines as it was lost in an accident soon after the change of denomination on 25 August with 265 hours to the airframe.
(National Naval Aviation Museum)

F3F-1 BuNo 0256 was among the few F3F-1s assigned to the Marines. This airframe is seen with the new codes introduced in July 1937 when VF-4M became VMF-2. In December 1937, BuNo 0256 was returned to the USN where it served with VF-4 and VF-3 and later at NAS Miami as advanced trainer. It was stricken from inventory at the end of January 1943.
(National Naval Aviation Museum)

XF3F-2

-

X: Experimental, **F:** Fighter, **3F:** Grumman Third type, **2:** Second model
Grumman third fighter type, prototype of the second model

Number of aircraft ordered:	**1**
Number of aircraft accepted:	**1**
Delivery dates:	*Jul.37*
Last stricken date:	*n/a*

Bu.No:
0452 (1)

The Grumman XF3F-2 was a variant proposed by Grumman in June 1936 as a development of the XF3F-1. The main change was the engine, a new 950-hp Wright R-1820 Cyclone. This engine installation required a redesign of the forward fuselage of the F3F-1 airframe. A three-blade propeller was also installed. The prototype, BuNo 0452, made its first flight on 21 July 1936 and immediately demonstrated very good performance with an increase of ten percent over that of the F3F-1.
Its card states the XF3F-2 was sent to the Naval Aircraft Factory in September 1937, where it was converted to a F3F-1 with a R-1535 engine, and returned to Anacostia in April 1938. Indeed, it seems that, comparing it with a F3F-2 production example, the XF3F-2 was a kind of hybrid and it was simpler and more economical to bring it back to F3F-1 standard than upgrade it to full F3F-2 standard. Later on, 0452 joined the fleet, being issued to VF-3 from May 1939, before serving briefly with VF-4 and ending its days as a trainer at Miami until the end of March 1943 when it was struck from the inventory.

Prototype XF3F-2 during a test flight. It was later converted to F3F-1 standard.

F3F-2

-

F: Fighter, **3F**: Grumman Third type, **2**: Second model
Grumman third fighter type, second model.

Number of aircraft ordered:	81
Number of aircraft accepted:	81
Delivery dates:	Nov.37
Last stricken date:	Nov.43

Bu.No:
0967/1047 (81)

A contract for 81 F3F-2s was signed in March 1937, enough to equip three squadrons. They differed from the prototype by incorporating a new rudder shape with increased area to compensate for the increased engine torque of the higher powered engine, a R-1820-22 Cyclone rated at 950-hp. A new canopy and windscreen were also installed.

The first unit to receive the F3F-2 was Fighting Squadron Six in November 1937. In the following months, Marine Fighting Squadron Two was the next to be equipped and was soon followed by the re-equipment of VMF-1. When the F2A and F4F were introduced into service, the F3F-2 was progressively withdrawn from frontline units, the last being VMF-2, which retired its last F3F-2 in October 1941. Once removed from fleet service, the F3F-2s were assigned to Training Command at various bases, mainly at Miami and Corpus Christi. When the Pearl Harbor attack occurred, eighteen and fourteen were serving at those USN training bases respectively. The type continued in this role until the airframes were time expired and retired. The last one, BuNo 0983, was struck from the inventory in November 1943.

> Side view of F3F-2 BuNo 0986 with VF-6 markings. As 6-F-7, this airframe was the mount of the Blue Section leader.

Three F3F-2s which saw service with Fighting Squadron Six, embarked on the USS *Enterprise* in 1938: BuNo 0969/6-F-2, BuNo 0983/6-F-4, aircraft of the White section leader and BuNo 0998/6-F-13, with the markings of the aircraft flown by the Green Section. Those three F3F-2s would join the Training Command to serve as advanced trainer. BuNo 0983 would the last F3F to be stricken off in November 1943 while BuNo 0969 was stricken in June 1942 and 0998 in May 1943.
The tail color is blue.
(National Naval Aviation Museum)

Fighting Squadron Six in flight leading the by the Black Section leader.

F3F-2 6-F-18 was the last aircraft of Fighting Squadron Six. The sixth section was given the color yellow. This number was assigned to BuNo 1003, an airframe that will end its career as an advanced trainer as many others. It was stricken in February 1943.
Marine Fighting Squadron Two was the first of the USMC squadrons to receive F3F-2s. Here leading BuNo 0973, followed by BuNos 0979 and 0977. Of those, two were lost on accident, BuNo 0973 in November 1940 and BuNo 0977 in March 1942. The latter was stricken with 1,490.8 hours to the airframe. *(National Naval Aviation Museum)*

Left, another view of BuNo 0977/2-MF-8 of the previous page. It belongs to Blue Section. Below F3F-2 BuNo 0994 of Green Section of VMF-2 in 1938. Later on it would serve at Corpus Christi as advanced trainer and was stricken from inventory following an accident in June 1942. *(National Naval Aviation Museum)*

Left, F3F-2 BuNo 0997 coded 2-MF-18 in 1938 (Yellow section). It later went to Corpus Christi where it served as advanced trainer until the end of 1942.

Marine Fighting Squadron One based at Quantico was the last of the three Marine squadrons to receive F3F-2s and replaced its ageing F4B4s in the spring of 1938. Both airframe BuNo 1009 above and BuNo 1014 below were later passed on to the Training Command as advanced trainers. They were removed from service respectively in February 1943 and December 1942. *(National Naval Aviation Museum)*

Two more F3F-2s of Marine Fighting Squadron One BuNo 1022 which was lost by accident shortly after Pearl Harbor. It was then serving as an advanced trainer at NAS Miami and below BuNo 1023 which ended its career as an advanced trainer as well but at Corpus Christi. *(National Naval Aviation Museum)*

As Brewster F2As and Grumman F4Fs became available from late 1940, F3Fs were progressively transferred to the Training Command. Here wearing individual numbers as codes, F3F-2s (and possibly some F3F-3s) are flying a right echelon formation.

XF3F-3

-

X: Experimental, **F:** Fighter, **3F:** Grumman Third type, **3:** Third model
Grumman third fighter type, prototype of the third model

Number of aircraft ordered: **1**
Number of aircraft accepted: **1** *(convertion from a F3F-2)*
Delivery dates: **Jan.39**
Last stricken date: **Mar.43**

Bu.No:
1031 (1)

In the summer of 1938, the future of the USN fighter was the monoplane. However, the concept was still rather new and the USN anticipated difficulties in the relevant programmes under way, the Brewster F2A and the Grumman F4F. At the same time, an additional carrier air group was being formed for the USS Wasp and the USN feared a critical aircraft shortage. To fill the gap, the F3F-3, an improved F3F-2, was proposed by Grumman. To this end, F3F-2 BuNo 1031, having already been delivered to the Navy, was returned to Grumman in May 1938 for modifications and became the XF3F-3.

Compared to the F3F-2, the XF3F-3 incorporated several aerodynamic refinements that included a redesigned wing leading edge, a tighter fitting cowling, deletion of the fuselage cowling vents and a redesigned windscreen similar to the XF4F-2. Unsurprisingly, the type was eventually accepted by the Navy after trials in January 1939.

The aircraft continued to serve as a test aircraft until July 1941 when it was sent to Corpus Christi to be incorporated in the large fleet of F3Fs already serving as advanced trainers. It seems that it kept its denomination until being stricken along with many other F3Fs on 31 March 1943.

Side view of the XF3F-3 seen in October 1938. Note the windshield similar to that used on the XF4F-2.

Prototype XF3F-3 seen from another angle showing the improvements on the leading edges and cowling and deletion of the fuselage cowling vents.

F3F-3

-

F: Fighter, **3F**: Grumman Third type, **3**: Third model
Grumman third fighter type, third model.

Number of aircraft ordered:	27
Number of aircraft accepted:	27
Delivery dates:	Jan.39/May.39
Last stricken date:	Jul.43

Bu.No:
1444/1471 (27)

In June 1938, the USN ordered 27 F3F-3s to equip one fighter squadron. This was the production model of the XF3F-3 that did not incorporate the XF4F-2 canopy, but reverted to the canopy used by the F3F-2.
The F3F-3s were delivered in the first semester of 1939 with the majority being assigned to VF-5 aboard the USS *Yorktown*. The others were assigned to other fighter squadrons to augment their fleets of F3F-2s, and two, BuNos 1462 and 1463, went to NAS Anacostia for general purpose work. In June 1941, VF-5 relinquished its F3F-3s for F4F-3s, marking the end of the Navy biplane fighter in frontline units. As with the previous F3F models, the surviving dash 3s found a second career as advanced trainers, mainly at Corpus Christi in Texas, while a few others served at NAS Miami in the same role. By Pearl Harbor, sixteen of them were still active at Corpus Christi (of the 22 still available to the USN). The withdrawal of the type began early in 1943, as the airframes reached their hour limits, and the process was completed in July 1943 when BuNo 1463 was stricken.

Side view of the second production F3F-3, BuNo 1445. It was the first F3F-3 to be assigned to VF-5. As many F3F-3s, it ended as advanced trainer and was stricken from the list in January 1943. *(National Naval Aviation Museum)*

The first three F3F-3s assigned to VF-5 flying in formation in November 1939. Flying with 1445/5-F-1 leading, 1446/5F-2 and 1447/5-F-3 are following. BuNos 1446 and 1447 continued their career as advanced trainer until December 1942 for 1447 and January 1943 for 1446.

Above, BuNo 1463 seen while serving at NAS Anacostia. In January 1942 it was sent to Corpus Christi to serve as advanced trainer. It was stricken in July 1943 and was the last F3F-3 in the inventory at that time. *(National Naval Aviation Museum)*

Below three F3F-3s flying in formation. They are serving here as advanced trainers at Corpus Christi, a recently commissioned station. In the previous years, it had been recommended to open a second air training station after NAS Miami. The first training flights were performed in May 1941. In the forefront, BuNo 1444 coded 13, the first F3F-3 built. It initially flew at NAS Anacostia before going to Corpus Christi. He was stricken in June 1943.
(National Naval Aviation Museum)

XF4F-1

Wildcat

X: Experimental, **F**: Fighter, **4F**: Grumman Fourth type, **1**: Initial model
Grumman fourth fighter type, prototype of the initial model

Number of aircraft ordered: -
Number of aircraft accepted: -
Delivery dates: -
Last stricken date: -

Bu.No:
-

In November of 1935, the USN was already looking for a successor to the F3F and released a request for proposals for a new carrier-based fighter. Grumman became one of the two contractors and submitted its XF4F-1, a biplane developed from the F3F-2, then in advanced development. However, the competitor, Brewster, submitted its XF2A-1, an all-metal monoplane with calculated performance figures far better than the Grumman offering. In late July 1936, at the manufacturer's suggestion, the Navy requested work on the XF4F-1 be terminated in favour of a new design, the XF4F-2, by amendment to the contract.

XF4F-2

Wildcat

X: Experimental, **F:** Fighter, **4F:** Grumman Fourth type, **2:** Second model
Grumman fourth fighter type, prototype of the second model

Number of aircraft ordered:	1
Number of aircraft accepted:	-
Delivery dates:	-
Last stricken date:	*n/a*

Bu.No:
0383 (1)

Following the amendment of the contract, Grumman completed the construction of the XF4F-2 in September 1937. The aircraft was now a mid-wing, full cantilever, all-metal design of semi-monocoque aluminium construction. It was powered by a 1050-hp Pratt & Whitney R-1830-66 and its armament consisted of two 0.30-in calibre machine guns firing through the propeller arc with the capability to carry two additional guns in the wings as well as a 100-lb bomb under each wing.
The first flight occurred on 2 September. The trials showed some flaws, and two mishaps were experienced, but all were solved with some configuration changes and improvements. Even though the XF4F-2 was faster than the XF2A-1 and XNF-1 in the competition, the USN eventually selected the F2A-1 as the winner in June 1938. The XF4F-2 was never accepted by the Navy and remained Grumman property throughout the trials. However, the USN felt the XF4F-2 had great potential and, in October 1938, Grumman received a Navy contract to convert the XF4F-2 into the XF4F-3.

Side view of the prototype XF4F-2 in its initial configuration.

Prototype XF4F-2 in its last configuration which had a longer-chord cowling and a larger carburetor intake than the initial configuration.

XF4F-3

Wildcat

X: Experimental, **F:** Fighter, **4F:** Grumman Fourth type, **3:** Third model
Grumman fourth fighter type, prototype of the third model

Number of aircraft ordered:	1
Number of aircraft accepted:	1
Delivery dates:	Jul.39
Last stricken date:	Jan.41

Bu.No:
0383 (1)

After its second accident of 11 April 1938, the remains of the XF4F-2 were sent to Grumman. In the meantime, the USN had chosen the XF2A-1, but asked Grumman to deliver a XF4F-3. The mods were completed early in 1939 and the first flight was made on 12 February 1939. It was armed with two 0.50-in calibre machine guns in the wings and two in the nose of 0.30-in calibre.

The XF4F-3 was now powered by a 1200-hp Pratt & Whitney R-1830-76 and was a bit longer than the XF4F-2. Additionally, wing dihedral was increased, as was the wingspan, and some aerodynamic refinements were also applied. However, the first flights revealed some lack of stability, and engine cooling problems, so further modifications were undertaken. The aircraft received a new tail and the cooling problems were solved. In August 1939, the trials were satisfactory enough to lead to an order for the USN. The aircraft was officially accepted and continued to fly for various experiments. In November 1940 it was used by VF-4 on the USS Ranger before being issued to VF-71 and VF-72 on the USS Wasp. It was eventually destroyed in a crash on 17 December 1940 and stricken the following month with 345.4 hours on the airframe.

Side view the XF4F-3 in its initial configuration.

The XF4F-3 was sent to the National Advisory Council on Aeronautics (NACA) facility at Langley, Virginia to test various propeller, spinner and cowl flap configurations.

F4F-3

Wildcat

F: Fighter, **4F**: Grumman Fourth type, **3**: Third model
Grumman fourth fighter type, third model

Number of aircraft ordered:	383
Number of aircraft accepted:	286
Delivery dates:	Aug.40/May.43
Last stricken date:	Dec.44

Bu.No:
1844/1845 (2), **1848/1897** (50), **2512/2538** (27), **3856/3874** (19), **3970/4057** (88),
12230/12329 (100)

In August 1939, the USN placed an order for 54 F4F-3s that were very close to the specifications of the XF4F-3, but with four 0.50-in calibre machine guns in the wings. This model would evaluate changes and receive modifications throughout the production phase. The first two Fighting Squadrons to be equipped were VF-4 and VF-72. This order was soon followed by others for a total of 188 ordered and, by Pearl Harbor, 176 were still in service, fully equipping eight squadrons, including two USMC units. The last order was placed in May 1942 for 100 aircraft, but these remained stateside to serve mainly as advanced trainers. In 1942, some were converted to F3F-3Ps while others were delivered as later F4F prototypes, like the F4F-3A or F4F-7.

By the end of December 1942, about 220 F4F-3s remained in the USN inventory serving in various operational units stateside, proving how furious the first year of the war in the Pacific had been. But, by the following summer, all surviving aircraft, with a few exceptions, were serving as advanced trainers, reinforced by the last batch of 100 ordered and delivered by Grumman (ex-F4F-3S). By 1 July 1944, this number had been reduced to about fifty F4F-3s and the type was eventually withdrawn from use at the end of 1944 with the last aircraft stricken on 31 December.

Side view of F4F-3 BuNo 1848 of Fighting Squadron Four in November 1940 at the time of the introduction into service. The space between the 4 and the dash was reserved to apply a 1 or 2 for either VF-41 either VF-42 and therefore the F4F-3 was here awaiting delivery. It was lost after a crash on the USS *Hornet* on 23 March 1942. *(National Naval Aviation Museum)*

Left, only a few F4F-3s received the pre-war markings including this one, BuNo 1850 of Fighting Squadron Forty-One of the USS Ranger. The '1' was yet to be applied on the fuselage. It was the aircraft of the Second Section with a white band. Note the small national markings insignia on the nose which was adopted in March of 1940. It would crash at sea on 17 November 1942 while serving with VMO-251.
(National Naval Aviation Museum)

Middle left, F4F-3 BuNo 2538 of VF-42. VF-42 was the redenomination of VS-41 on 1 March 1941.
(National Naval Aviation Museum)

Below a F4F-3 with the new camouflage and marking of January 1942. This aircraft belongs to Fighting Squadron Two.
(National Naval Aviation Museum)

Two F4F-3s of Fighting Squadron Three flying over the sea during a combat air patrol in April 1942 with BuNo 3976 in the forefront and BuNo 3986 acting as wingman. The squadron used the Wildcat until July of 1943. *(National Naval Aviation Museum)*

Above a F4F-3 of VF-8 on patrol during early 1942.
Below a F4F-3 in patrol during late 1942 with the extra-large national roundel.
(National Naval Aviation Museum)

Above also taken on patrol a F4F-3 coded F-22 in the middle of 1942.
Below, by the end of 1943 many F4F-3s were serving as advanced trainer in Stateside. Here survivors of the early Pacific war cruises, BuNo 1845 and Bu No 3990, flying in formation.

F4F-3A

Wildcat

F: Fighter, **4F**: Grumman Fourth type, **3**: Third model, **A**: Miscellaneous modification
Grumman fourth fighter type, third model with miscellaneous modification

Number of aircraft ordered:	**95**
Number of aircraft accepted:	**95**
Delivery dates:	**Mar.41/May.41**
Last stricken date:	**Aug.44**

Bu.No:
3875/3969 (95)

In fear of a shortage of the two-stage supercharged engines powering the F4F-3, the USN ordered 95 F4F-3As, the production version of the XF4F-6, powered by a 1200-hp Pratt & Whitney R-1830-90. They were actually diverted from the third F4F-3 order and were otherwise similar to the F4F-3. Thirty of them were almost immediately sent to Greece, but eventually ended up in British hands after Greece surrendered. The remaining aircraft entered service with VMF-111 in April and by Pearl Harbor the F4F-3A was also serving with VF-3, VF-6, VF-5 and VF-8.
Participating in the first stages of the Pacific War, they were progressively withdrawn from frontline units. At least one was converted to a F4F-3P in 1942 while the others continued to serve with various stateside units. In 1943, the bulk of the survivors were stricken, leaving eight still on USN charge by 1 January 1944, but, by the end of the year, none remained in USN hands.

This F4F-3A, BuNo 3905 was the first production F4F-3A delivered to the Navy in April 1941. The first thirty F4F-3s went to Greece.
(National Naval Aviation Museum)

Grumman F4F-3A BuNo 3960 seen shortly after its delivery to the US Navy on 20 May 1941. It was stricken in August 1943. *(National Naval Aviation Museum)*

A section of Wildcats of Fighting Squadron Five (USS Ranger) flying in formation before the war. All are painted in the pre-war NS Light Grey with the small national insignia. The aircraft leading is a F4F3A (BuNo 3927) but the squadron was mainly equipped with the F4F-3 in December 1941. BuNo 3927 was stricken from inventory in March 1943. *National Naval Aviation Museum)*

Below, prior to initial delivery to the USN, the Greek Purchasing Commission ordered 30 F4F-3s in May 1940. The aircraft were en route to Greece at the time of their surrender in April of 1941. Well before discussions with the British had been engaged and an exchange agreed for those F4F-3As for another type to be supplied to the Greek from British stocks in the Middle East, possibly Tomahawks. The Greek surrender stopped the discussions and the F4F-3A entered in Fleet Air Arm service under the designation of Martlet Mk III. Note the former BuNo painted on the fuselage.

F4F-3P

Wildcat

F: Fighter, **4F**: Grumman Fourth type, **3**: Third model, **P**: Photographic version
Grumman fourth fighter type, photographic version of the third model

Number of aircraft ordered:	20 (conversion)
Number of aircraft accepted:	20
Delivery dates:	Feb.42/Mar.43
Last stricken date:	Aug.44

Bu.No:
1849, 1852, 1856, 1865, 1867, 1870, 1871, 1872, 1875, 1880, 1894, 2512, 2517, 2524, 2526, 2530, 2537, 3918, 3985, 3997

If we believe the movement cards, the USN modified nineteen F4F-3s and one F4F-3A for reconnaissance missions. This was done by removing the reserve fuel tank, behind the pilot, but retaining the wing armament. One camera was mounted in the lower fuselage aft of the main fuel tank. The first conversions took place in February and March 1942 with some aircraft being converted, on a non-regular basis, until March 1943 to make up for attrition.

The F4F-3P saw limited service primarily in the Solomons during the fierce Guadalcanal campaign in 1942-1943. The main user was Marine Observation Squadron 251 (VMO-251) based in the New Hebrides. The aircraft served with operational squadrons until the summer of 1943. By that time only eleven remained on charge. Their subsequent usage is not known for certain, but they appeared in the US inventory until the end of August 1944.

A F4F-3P of VMO-251 under the a makeshift hangar at Espititu Santo in the New Hebrides.
(National Naval Aviation Museum)

F4F-3S

Wildcatfish

F: Fighter, **4F**: Grumman Third type, **3**: Third model, **S**: Seaplane
Grumman fourth fighter type, seplane version of the third model

Number of aircraft ordered:	**101**
Number of aircraft accepted:	**1** (conversion)
Delivery dates:	*n/a*
Last stricken date:	**Aug.44**

Bu.No:
4038 (1), *12230/12329 (100) canx*

The F4F-3S project arose in the autumn of 1942 after US forces encountered float fighters like the 'Rufe' (A6M-2N). These aircraft were used with some success and had respectable performance. They were useful where landing strips were not adequate and were seen as an effective stop-gap until infrastructure for land-based fighters could be built. Encountering the same problems as the Japanese, the USN tried to copy the concept using the F4F-3.

One F4F-3 (BuNo 4038) was sent to Edo Corporation for modification. It first flew on 28 February 1943. Some directional stability issues arose and led to the installation of a large ventral fin at the extreme lower fuselage. Overall performance was disappointing. However, when the first flight took place, the need for such aircraft had considerably diminished and no production aircraft were built. The order for 100 examples was eventually delivered as standard F4F-3s for use as trainers.

The sole F4F-3A taking-off in open water near NAS Norfolk. The aircraft is here shown without the large ventral fin that was later added to improve directional stability. *(National Naval Aviation Museum)*

Above, the F4F-3S as seen in is initial configuration without the large ventral fin and below seen after the installation of the ventral fin located under the aft fuselage. The aircraft retained the four-gun armament and also carried a bomb rack under each wing.
(National Naval Aviation Museum)

XF4F-4

Wildcat

X: Experimental, **F**: Fighter, **4F**: Grumman Fourth type, **4**: Fourth model
Grumman fourth fighter type, prototype of the fourth model

Number of aircraft ordered:	**1**
Number of aircraft accepted:	**1**
Delivery dates:	**Jan.42**
Last stricken date:	**Jan.43**

Bu.No:
1897 (1)

To save space on an aircraft carrier, Grumman was asked to try to install a set of hydraulically folding wings. A contract was signed for this purpose in March 1940 and the last F4F-3 of the initial order, BuNo 1897, was diverted from the production line and modified to become the XF4F-4.

It was not as easy as first thought as some changes to the aircraft's structure, to accommodate the folding wing assembly, had to be incorporated. That took a year and the XF4F-4 flew for the first time on 15 April 1941. Tests were successful and led to a production version. Trials continued and the XF4F-4 was later delivered to VF-42, and then VF-3 (with which it was serving when Pearl Harbor took place). It was officially accepted in January 1942 and from April 1942 served at the ACTG (Advanced Carrier Training Group). It was lost after a crash on 30 January 1943.

Prototype XF4F-4 was the only Wildcat to have hydraulically-actuated folding wings at the production version (F4F-4) had manually folded wings.

F4F-4

Wildcat

F: Fighter, **4F**: Grumman Fourth type, **4**: Fourth model
Grumman fourth fighter type, fourth model

Number of aircraft ordered:	**1171**
Number of aircraft accepted:	**1169**
Delivery dates:	**Nov.41/Dec.42**
Last stricken date:	**Feb.46**

Bu.No:
4058/4098 (41), **5030/5262** (223), **01991/02152** (162), **03385/03544** (160), **11655/12227** (573)

Following successful testing of the XF4F-4, the USN initially ordered the F4F-4 in June 1941 as an amendment to the last F4F-3 contract. Production commenced before Pearl Harbor, but only one aircraft had been accepted by the Navy by that time. The main difference to the prototype was the wings were folded manually. The engine was a 1200-hp R-1830-86 and, compared to the F4F-3, the armament was increased to six 0.50-in calibre machine guns (four close to the wing fold and two further outboard). Armour protection was also improved. When the US entered into war, more orders were placed, the last taking place in May 1942.The first squadrons to operate the F4F-4 were VF-6 and VF-8 deployed on the USS *Enterprise*, but the first combat occurred during the Battle of Midway in June 1942. The F4F-4 became the backbone of the USN fighter force and participated in all of the following battles, but suffered heavy losses in return. By 31 December 1942, with the delivery of the last F4F-4, about 820 were still in service, a number that decreased to 445 one year later. At that time, it was still serving in some Composite Squadrons (VC-11, VC-20, VC-27, VC-33, VC-75, VC-77, VC-81) stateside, having been replaced by the F6F and FM on the frontline.

The F4F-4 continued to serve mainly as a trainer throughout 1944, but the aircraft were progressively withdrawn during the year, only one being kept in the USN records after 30 November 1944. The very last one, BuNo 4058, was stricken on 28 February 1946.

F4F-4 BuNo 4084 of Fighting Squadron Forty-One was accepted by the Navy on 12 January 1942 and is seen soon after with the extra-large US roundel.

A F4F-4 of Fighting Squadron Six with wings unfolded on the USS *Entreprise* in April 1942. *(National Naval Aviation Museum)*

F4F-4s pictured on one of the aircraft elevators on board the carrier USS *Enterprise* (CV 6) with wings folded. *(National Naval Aviation Museum)*

Below, a F4F-4 of VF-6 on the flight deck of the carrier USS *Enterprise* on 10 April 1942 *(National Naval Aviation Museum)*

A F4F-4 of Fighting Squadron Three has its engine being warmed-up by a mechanic in the beginning of 1942. *(National Naval Aviation Museum)*

Above, a group of mechanics inspect the engine of a F4F-4 of Armed Scouting Squadron Thirty (VGS-30) at NAS Norfolk in September 1942.
Below, F4F-4 Wildcat of Marine Fighting Squadron (VMF) 121 at Camp Kearney, located on the site of the future Naval Air Station (NAS) Miramar, California being inspected.

Above, Marine Wildcats line the taxiway of Henderson Field at Guadalcanal in November 1943. The F4F-4 was at that time at the end of its operational use. Below, a F4F-4 of VF-9 (coded 25) preparing for take-off from USS *Ranger* in November 1942. Note the large Yellow circle used for Operation Torch.
(National Naval Aviation Museum)

F4F-4s of either VF-41 or VF-9 line the deck edge aboard USS *Ranger* testing their guns prior to the beginning of Operation Torch. *(National Naval Aviation Museum)*

Below, USMC F4F-4s on patrol off Guadalcanal in April 1943. *(National Naval Aviation Museum)*

F4F-4A

Wildcat

F: Fighter, **4F**: Grumman Fourth type, **4**: Fourth model, **A**: Miscellaneous modification
Grumman fourth fighter type, fourth model with miscellaneous modification

Number of aircraft ordered: -
Number of aircraft accepted: -
Delivery dates: -
Last stricken date: -

Bu.No:
-

This designation was allocated to a proposed version of the F4F-4 powered by a Pratt & Whitney R-1830-90 engine similar to the F4F-3. The need for it never materialised.

F4F-4B

Martlet/Wildcat

F: Fighter, **4F**: Grumman Fourth type, **4**: Fourth model, **B**: British specification
Grumman fourth fighter type, fourth model with British specifications

Number of aircraft ordered:	**220**
Number of aircraft accepted:	**220**
Delivery dates:	**Feb.42/Nov.42**
Last stricken date:	**Jan.46**

Bu.No:
0031/0250 (220)

The F4F-4B was the version supplied to the British under the Lend Lease Act and was powered by a 1240-hp Wright Cyclone G-205A (R-1820-40). The British serials allocated to this model were FN100 to FN319. It became the Martlet Mk.IV, but changed to the Wildcat Mk.IV from 1 January 1944.
The aircraft served until the end of war even though they only flew as advanced trainers during the later stages. By VE-Day about thirty were still flying with the Fleet Air Arm, but, with the end of war, they were soon retired and scrapped.

Martlet Mk IV FN100, the first of its kind. It served operationally with No. 896 and 890 Squadrons of the Fleet Air Arm (FAA) before ending its days in 19444 with No. 738 Squadron, a FAA second-line unit.

F4F-4P

Wildcat

F: Fighter, **4F**: Grumman Fourth type, **4**: Fourth model, **P**: Photographic version
Grumman fourth fighter type, photographic version of the fourth model

Number of aircraft ordered: n/k
Number of aircraft accepted: 4 (at least)
Delivery dates: Apr.42/Aug.42
Last stricken date: Aug.44

Bu.No:
known aircraft: 4082, 5159, 5160, 11663

According to the cards, four F4F-4s were converted for photographic work as F4F-4Ps, possibly to reinforce the diminishing F4F-3P fleet. The number of conversions, however, could be higher. They were used alongside the earlier aircraft and there are traces of them with Fighting Squadron 41 in 1942 and Photographic Squadron Two (VD-2) in 1943 at Norfolk. All examples were gone by the end of the summer of 1944.

One of the few F4F-4Ps seen in flight in October 1943 with the codes of the VD-2. *(National Naval Aviation Museum)*

XF4F-5

Wildcat

X: Experimental, **F**: Fighter, **4F**: Grumman Fourth type, **5**: Fifth model
Grumman fourth fighter type, prototype of the fifth model

Number of aircraft ordered:	**2**
Number of aircraft accepted:	**2**
Delivery dates:	**Jul.40**
Last stricken date:	**Jan.46**

Bu.No:
1846 & 1847 (2)

The XF4F-5 was developed following persistent problems with the R-1830's two-stage supercharger. Therefore, an alternative powerplant was considered, a 1200-hp Wright R-1820-40 Cyclone with a single-stage supercharger, and the airframe received the XF4F-5 denomination. Two F4F-3s, BuNos 1846 and 1847, were retained by Grumman to be modified. The XF4F-5 made its maiden flight in June 1940, but no production order followed. The two aircraft were accepted by the Navy in July 1940. Evaluation proved the XF4F-5 had performance close to the F4F-3 up to 15,000 feet.

The two XF4F-5s continued to fly for the Navy as engine test beds. Both had long careers with the USN as 1857 was stricken in August 1945 and 1846 in January 1946.

The XF4F-5 during its acceptance trials in July 1940. The two prototypes appeared externally similar to the G-36A/Martlet Mk I the export version of the F4F-3. Both aircraft would be modified again near the end of 1942 with new engines. *(National Naval Aviation Museum)*

XF4F-6

Wildcat

X: Experimental, **F**: Fighter, **4F**: Grumman Fourth type, **6**: Sixth model
Grumman fourth fighter type, prototype of the sixth model

Number of aircraft ordered:	**1**
Number of aircraft accepted:	**1**
Delivery dates:	**Nov.40**
Last stricken date:	**May.42**

Bu.No:
7031 (1)

Based on the F4F-3, the XF4F-6 actually served as the prototype for the F4F-3A. It was powered by a 1200-hp Pratt & Whitney R-1830-S3C4G radial engine with a single-stage, two-speed supercharger. It made its first flight on 11 October 1940 and was accepted by the Navy the following month.
As for the aircraft, after the USN had ordered the F4F-3A, it continued to serve in a variety of evaluation roles until destroyed in a crash on 25 May 1942, sadly killing the pilot.

Prototype XF4F-6 was equipped of the export variant of the R-1830-90 and served as test bed for the this engine. The export variant became the Martlet III for the British Fleet Air Arm while for the USN, it would become the F4F-3A. *(National Naval Aviation Museum)*

F4F-7

Wildcat

F: Fighter, **4F**: Grumman Fourth type, **7**: Seventh model
Grumman fourth fighter type, seventh model

Number of aircraft ordered:	121
Number of aircraft accepted:	21
Delivery dates:	Jan.42/Feb.43
Last stricken date:	Aug.44

Bu.No:
5263/5283 (21)

The F4F-7 was developed after the USN recognised the need for a long-range reconnaissance aircraft well before the attack on Pearl Harbor. In January 1941, primary work was carried out based on the F4F-3 airframe. The modifications consisted of removing the guns, wing racks and gun sight, the fitting of a rounded windscreen similar to what was installed on early production aircraft before the adoption of the flat panel armoured version, and the installation of two cameras in place of the 27-US gallon aft fuselage tank of the F4F-3. The non-folding wings could house 555 US gallons of fuel, and two oil tanks were installed forward of the pilot. Before the work could be done on the F4F-3, the USN asked Grumman to perform the conversion on the F4F-4 airframe and in May 1942, with the last Wildcat order, 100 F4F-7s were anticipated. In the meantime, 21 aircraft were ordered as F4F-7s and were diverted from existing orders. The first F4F-7 was flown on 30 December 1941 and delivery began the following month. Later on, since the requirement was smaller than initially anticipated, the contract for 100 F4F-7s was cancelled and the contract amended for the F4F-3S and, eventually, the F4F-3. Some F4F-7s saw action over Guadalcanal with VMO-251. The F4F-7 served primarily with Marine Observation Squadron 251, but each time in small numbers as not all were shipped out overseas. The rest served stateside and, in the end, the F4F-7 saw little action. By 31 December 1943, fourteen were still in the inventory, but the last surviving aircraft were stricken on 31 August 1944.

F4F-7 BuNo 5274 parked at the Grumman factory before to be delivered to the Navy in September 1942. The number of F4F-7s accepted by the USN seems to have been higher than the number commonly agreed. *(National Naval Aviation Museum)*

Opposite side of BuNo 5274. (National Naval Aviation Museum)

10167

XF4F-8

Wildcat

X: Experimental, **F**: Fighter, **4F**: Grumman Fourth type, **8**: Eighth model
Grumman fourth fighter type, prototype of the eighth model

Number of aircraft ordered:	**2**
Number of aircraft accepted:	**2**
Delivery dates:	**Dec.42**
Last stricken date:	**Dec.44**

Bu.No: 12228 & 12229

The XF4F-8 was developed after the need for a fighter to operate from small escort carriers arose. This class of ship would reach the fleet in large numbers in 1943. At that time the F6F and the F4U were in high demand for both the USN and the USMC. The F4F was still a potent aircraft despite its role being taken over by the Hellcat and the Corsair. Therefore, the USN asked Grumman to work on a lightweight variant of the Wildcat that was more compatible with the small escort carriers. This was designated the XF4F-8 and two prototypes were ordered, the last F4F-4 contract being amended for this.
The XF4F-8 made its initial flight on 8 November 1942 and was powered by a 1350-hp Wright R-1820-56. The armament remained unchanged and there were various improvements compared to the F4F-4. Externally, the main difference was the vertical fin and rudder that was increased in size to counteract the more powerful engine's torque on the second prototype. The prototypes were accepted by the Navy in December 1942 and the production version was taken over by Eastern Aircraft Division as the **FM-2**.

The first XF4F-8 BuNo 12228 showing the new cowling, the main external difference to the previous Wildcat models. The tail if the same as the one installed on the F4F-3/4. *(National Naval Aviation Museum)*

Side view of the first XF4F-8 (BuNo 12228) and below the second XF4F-8 (BuNo 12229) with the new tail to counter the torque generated by the new engine and the extra 150 hp. This tail would be adopted for the FM-2. *(National Naval Aviation Museum)*

XF5F-1

Skyrocket

X: Experimental **F**: Fighter, **5F**: Grumman Fifth type, **1**: Initial model
Grumman fifth fighter type, prototype of the initial model.

Number of aircraft ordered: 1
Number of aircraft accepted: 1
Delivery dates: Jul.44
Last stricken date: Oct.44

Bu.No:
1442 (1)

The Grumman XF5F Skyrocket was a prototype of a twin-engine shipboard fighter interceptor. The USN ordered one prototype from Grumman on 30 June 1938 with the designation XF5F-1. The aircraft had a unique appearance: The forward 'nose' of the fuselage did not extend forward of the wing. Provision was made for two 23 mm (0.906-in) Madsen cannons as armament. The aircraft flew for the first time on 1 April 1940, but some flaws soon appeared obliging Grumman to modify the aircraft. The new XF5F-1 became available in July 1941, but, despite the modifications, little improvement was noted. The prototype continued to be evaluated and was eventually accepted by the Navy in July 1944. However, in the meantime, the Grumman twin-engine XF7F-1 had made its first flight and was proving much more promising. The XF5F-1 suffered several minor accidents until a final one that led to the write off of the aircraft in October 1944. It had flown 156 hours since its maiden flight.

The unique XF5F-1 seen after the modifications undertaken after its initial flight. The modifications were made to the prototype including reduction in the height of the cockpit canopy, revising the armament installation to four 0.5 in (12.7 mm) machine guns in place of the cannon, redesign of the engine nacelles, adding spinners to the propellers, and extending the fuselage forward of the wing.

Three views of the XF5F-1 in its initial configuration

USN AIRCRAFT 1922-1962

Vol. 1:
Type Designation Letter
'A'
(Pt-1)

Phil H. LISTEMANN

USN AIRCRAFT 1922-1962

Vol. 2:
Type Designation Letter
'A'
(Pt-2)

Phil H. LISTEMANN

USN AIRCRAFT 1922-1962

Vol.3:
Type Designation Letters
'A' (Pt-3) & 'B'

Phil H. LISTEMANN

USN AIRCRAFT 1922-1962

Vol.4:
Type Designation Letters
'BF', 'BT' & 'F' (Pt-1)

Phil H. LISTEMANN

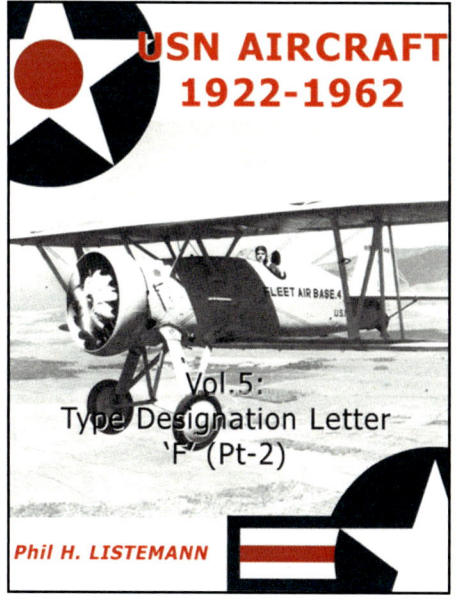

USN AIRCRAFT 1922-1962

Vol.5:
Type Designation Letter
'F' (Pt-2)

Phil H. LISTEMANN

USN AIRCRAFT 1922-1962

Vol.6:
Type Designation Letter
'F' (Pt-3)

Phil H. LISTEMANN

SQUADRONS!
No.3

Fighter Leaders
of the RAF, RAAF, RCAF, RNZAF & SAAF in WW2

USN AIRCRAFT
1922-1962

Vol.4:
Type Designation Letters
'BF', 'BT' & 'F' (Pt-1)

RAF, Dominion & Allied Squadrons
at War:
Study, History and Statistics

No.137 Squadron
1941 - 1945

Compiled by
Phil H. Listemann
with
Chris Thomas

Volume I
Phil H. Listemann

Fighter Leaders
of the RAF, RAAF, RCAF, RNZAF & SAAF in WW2

Volume III
Phil H. Listemann

SQUADRONS!
No.10

The North American
Mustang Mk. IV
in Western Europe

www.RAF-IN-COMBAT.com

- USN Aircraft 1922-1962 -
- Squadrons! -
- RAF, Dominion and Allied squadrons at War -
- Allied Wings -
- Famous squadrons of WW2 -
- Fighter Leaders -

RAF, Dominion & Allied Squadron
at War:
Study, History and Statistics

No.131 (County of Kent) Squadron
1941 - 1945

Famous Commonwealth Squadrons of WW2

No.453 (R.A.A.F.) Squadron
1941-1945
Buffalo, Spitfire

Phil H. Listemann

ALLIED WINGS

No.19
The English Electric CANBERRA
B(I).8
Phil H. Listemann

ALLIED WINGS

No.18
The Supermarine SPITFIRE
F.24
Phil H. Listemann

Made in the USA
Columbia, SC
27 October 2022